Human Body Experiments

Using Fingerprints, Hair, Muscles, and More

One Hour or Less Science Experiments

ROBERT GARDNER

Enslow Publishers, Inc.
40 Industrial Road
Box 398
Berkeley Heights, NJ 07922
USA

http://www.enslow.com

Library of Congress Cataloging-in-Publication Data

Gardner, Robert, 1929-
     Human body experiments using fingerprints, hair, muscles, and more : one hour or less science experiments / Robert Gardner.
          p. cm. — (Last-minute science projects)
     Summary: "Quick science experiments using the human body"— Provided by publisher.
     Includes index.
     ISBN 978-0-7660-3958-2
     1. Human physiology—Experiments—Juvenile literature. 2. Human body—Experiments—Juvenile literature. I. Title.
     QP37.G3595 2013
     612.0072—dc23

                              2011015585

Future editions

Paperback ISBN 978-1-4644-0147-3

ePUB ISBN 978-1-4645-1054-0

PDF ISBN 978-1-4646-1054-7

Printed in the United States of America

032012 Lake Book Manufacturing, Inc., Melrose Park, IL

10 9 8 7 6 5 4 3 2 1

To Our Readers: We have done our best to make sure all Internet Addresses in this book were active and appropriate when we went to press. However, the author and the publisher have no control over and assume no liability for the material available on those Internet sites or on other Web sites they may link to. Any comments or suggestions can be sent by e-mail to comments@enslow.com or to the address on the back cover.

✪ Enslow Publishers, Inc., is committed to printing our books on recycled paper. The paper in every book contains 10% to 30% post-consumer waste (PCW). The cover board on the outside of each book contains 100% PCW. Our goal is to do our part to help young people and the environment too!

Illustration Credits: © 2011 by Stephen Rountree (www.rountreegraphics.com), pp. 9, 15 (a), 17, 19, 23, 25, 27, 29, 31, 39; Enslow Publishers, Inc., p. 35 (a); Kenneth G. Rainis, pp. 15 (b), 21; LifeART image copyright 1988 Lippincott Williams & Wilkins. All rights reserved, p. 37; Stephen F. Delisle, pp. 13 (a), 43; Tom LaBaff, pp. 11, 13 (b), 33, 35 (b), 41.

Cover Photos: All photos are Shutterstock.com except for the barrette © 2009 Jupiter Images Corporation.

Contents

LAST MINUTE Science Projects

🎗 Contains ideas for more science fair projects

Are You Running Late?

Maybe you have a science project due tomorrow and you've put it off until now. What can you do? This book is here to help! You will find human body experiments that you can do in one hour or less. In fact, some of them can be done in 30 minutes, others in 15 minutes, and some in as little as five minutes.

Even if you have plenty of time to prepare for your next science project or science fair or are just looking for some fun science experiments, you can enjoy this book, too.

Each experiment is followed by a "Keep Exploring" section. There you will find ideas for projects or experiments in which the details are left to you. You can design and carry out your own experiments, under adult supervision, when you have more time.

Sometimes you may need a partner to help you. Work with someone who likes to do experiments as much as you do. Then you will both enjoy what you are doing. If any safety issues or danger is involved in doing an experiment, you will be warned. In some cases, you will be asked to work with an adult. Don't take any chances that could lead to an injury.

Like any good scientist, you will find it useful to record your ideas, notes, data, and conclusions in a notebook. You will be able to refer to things you have done, which will help you with future experiments.

The Scientific Method

Different sciences use different ways of experimenting. Depending on the problem, one method is likely to be better than another. Designing a new medicine for heart disease and finding evidence of water on Mars require different experiments.

Even with these differences, most scientists use the scientific method. This includes: making an observation, coming up with a question, making a hypothesis (a possible answer to the question) and a prediction (an if-then statement), designing and conducting an experiment, analyzing results, drawing conclusions, and deciding if the hypothesis is true or false. Scientists share their results. They publish articles in science journals.

Once you have a question, you can make a hypothesis. Your hypothesis is a possible answer to the question (what you think will happen). For example, you might hypothesize that a person's heart will beat faster after he or she runs for ten minutes. Then you test your hypothesis.

In most cases, you should do a controlled experiment. This means having two groups that are treated the same except for the thing being tested. That thing is called a variable. To test the hypothesis above, you might listen to the hearts of two people while they are both sitting and quiet. You would then have one person run for ten minutes while the other continues to sit. You would listen to their hearts again. If the heart of the runner is beating faster while the other person's heart rate is unchanged, you would say that your hypothesis is true.

The results of one experiment often lead to another question. Or they may send you off in another direction. Whatever the results, something can be learned from every experiment!

Science Fairs

All the investigations in this book contain ideas that might lead you to a science fair project. However, judges at science fairs do not reward projects or experiments that are simply copied from a book. For example, a labeled diagram of a human skeleton would not impress most judges; however, a unique experiment to measure human power might gain their attention.

Science fair judges tend to reward creative thought and imagination. It is difficult to be creative or imaginative unless you are really interested in your project. Therefore, try to choose an investigation that excites you. And before you jump into a project, consider, too, your own talents and the cost of the materials you will need.

If you decide to use an experiment or idea found in this book for a science fair, find ways to modify or extend it. This should not be difficult. As you do investigations, you will get new ideas. You will think of questions that experiments can answer. The experiments will make great science fair projects because the ideas are your own and are interesting to you.

Your Notebook

Your notebook, as any scientist will tell you, is a valuable possession. It should contain ideas you may have as you experiment, sketches you may draw, calculations you make, and hypotheses you may suggest. It should include a description of every experiment you do and the data you record, such as voltages, currents, resistors, weights, and so on. It should also contain the results of your experiments, graphs, and conclusions.

Safety First

1. Do any experiments or projects, whether from this book or of your own design, under the adult supervision of a science teacher or other knowledgeable adult.

2. Read all instructions carefully before proceeding with a project. If you have questions, check with your supervisor before going any further.

3. Always wear safety goggles when doing experiments that could cause particles to enter your eyes. Tie back long hair and wear shoes that cover your feet completely.

4. Do not eat or drink while experimenting. Never taste substances being used (unless instructed to do so).

5. Use only alcohol-based thermometers. Older thermometers may contain mercury, which is a dangerous substance. It is dangerous to touch mercury or breathe mercury vapor, and such thermometers have been banned in many states. If you have a mercury thermometer in the house, ask an adult if it can be taken to a local thermometer exchange location.

6. Maintain a serious attitude while conducting experiments. Never engage in horseplay or play practical jokes.

7. At the end of every activity, clean all materials used and put them away. Then wash your hands thoroughly with soap and water.

One Hour or Less

Here are some experiments with the human body that you can do in one hour or less. You don't have any time to lose, so let's get started!

1 Is the Human Arm a Lever?

What's the Plan?

Let's find out why your arm is a lever. Figure 1a shows how the human arm lifts a weight. Figure 1b shows what scientists call a third-class lever. With a third-class lever, the load (weight lifted), W, is farther from the fulcrum, f, than the lifting force, F. A shovel (Figure 1c) is a third-class lever, and so is the human arm.

What You Do

1. Make a model of the human arm. Ask an adult to support the end of a yardstick at the edge of a bench or table. The end of the yardstick will be the lever's fulcrum (the arm's elbow). See Figure 1d.

2. Using string, attach a spring balance that can measure at least two pounds to the yardstick at the 12-inch mark. (The spring balance will measure the "arm's" lifting force.)

3. Use a strong rubber band or string to attach a one-pound weight (the weight the "arm" will lift) to the yardstick at the 24-inch mark.

WHAT YOU NEED:

- yardstick
- bench or table
- string
- spring balance that can measure at least two pounds
- strong rubber band or string
- one-pound weight

8

4. With what force must you lift with the spring scale to raise the one-pound weight?

What's Going On?

It probably took a lifting force of about two pounds to lift the one-pound weight. For any lever, the lifting force, F, times its distance, d, from the fulcrum equals the weight lifted, W, times its distance, D, from the fulcrum. In mathematical form: $F \times d = W \times D$.

As you can see from Figure 1a, the biceps muscle must exert a force much larger than the weight it lifts. The muscle's attachment is close to the fulcrum (elbow).

Keep Exploring—If You Have More Time!

- What are first- and second-class levers? Do experiments with them to see why they are useful machines. Are all human-body levers third class?

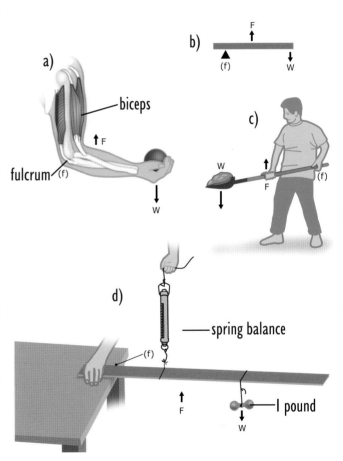

Figure 1. a) The human arm: a third-class lever. The biceps exerts an upward force, F, on the lower arm that lifts the weight, W. The elbow acts as a fulcrum, f. b) A diagram of a third-class lever. Notice that the lifting force, F, is closer to the fulcrum, f, than the weight lifted, W. c) A shovel is a third-class lever. d) A model of the human arm, a third-class lever.

2 Clothes to Keep Your Body Warm or Cool

What's the Plan?

Let's find out how choosing clothes of the right color can help you cope with the weather.

What You Do

1. Choose two socks, one dark (black or navy) and one white, made of the same material and having approximately the same weight.

2. Put a thermometer in the dark sock. Put an identical thermometer in the white sock. Hold the socks in place with rubber bands. The two thermometers should show temperatures that are very nearly the same.

3. Place both socks and their thermometers side by side in bright sunlight in front of a window or under a heat lamp (Figure 2). In warm weather, they can be placed outside in the sunlight.

4. Record the temperature inside each sock at five-minute intervals until you can reach a conclusion.

WHAT YOU NEED:

- 2 socks, one dark (black or navy), one white, made of the same material and having approximately the same weight
- 2 household thermometers
- bright sunlight or a heat lamp
- notebook and pencil
- clock or watch
- rubber bands

What's Going On?

You probably found that the dark sock became warmer than the white sock. Light-colored clothing and other light-colored matter reflect much of the light energy that strikes them. Dark clothes and other dark matter absorb much of the light energy that falls on them. The absorbed energy is changed to heat.

To stay warm in cold, sunny weather, it helps if you wear dark clothing to absorb the sun's energy. To stay cool in warm, sunny weather, you should wear light-colored clothing to reflect the sun's energy.

Keep Exploring—If You Have More Time!

- Paint the outside and inside of a tin can with flat black paint. When the paint is dry, fill the can and an identical shiny can with hot tap water. Put identical thermometers in the two cans. Record the temperatures every five minutes. Which can loses heat faster?

- Do experiments to show how sweating helps the human body cope with hot weather.

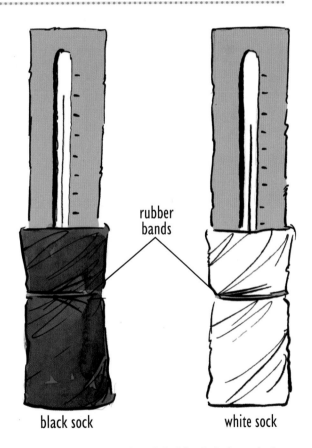

rubber bands

black sock

white sock

Figure 2. How does the color of clothing help keep the human body warm or cool?

3 Two Types of Reflexes

What's the Plan?
Let's look at two human body reflexes.

What You Do

WHAT YOU NEED:
- a partner
- table
- large, plastic kitchen spatula
- flashlight

1. Have a partner sit on a table with his legs relaxed, hanging over the table's edge.

2. Unless you have a doctor's rubber hammer, use a large, plastic kitchen spatula to test your partner's "knee-jerk" or patellar reflex (Figure 3a). Strike your partner's leg just below the knee cap (patella) and above the top of the tibia (lower leg bone). The reflex response is the contraction of the upper leg's quadriceps muscle, which pulls the lower leg upward.

3. Can your friend prevent the reflex by tightening his or her leg muscles?

4. Examine the pupils of your partner's eyes in normal light (Figure 3b).

5. Have your partner close his or her eyes for at least one minute.

6. When the eyes open, notice the size of the pupils. Watch the pupils shrink in response to the light.

7. Shine a flashlight into one eye of your partner. What happens to the size of the pupil? The pupil of the other eye responds in the same way.

8. Can your partner prevent the pupils from responding to changes in light intensity?

What's Going On?

Many reflexes, such as the pupil's response to light, breathing, and digestion, are controlled by nerves of the autonomic nervous system. These reflexes cannot be controlled by a human's will. Others, such as the patellar reflex, can be controlled by voluntary action.

Keep Exploring—If You Have More Time

- What is the ciliospinal reflex? The blinking reflex? Can you produce them with your partner?

- Compare the time for the patellar reflex stimulus to work with the voluntary response to the command "kick your leg upward." How can you explain any difference in the response times?

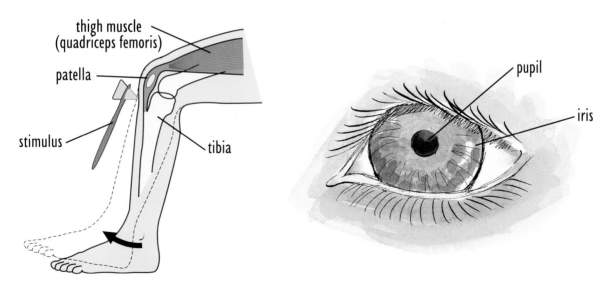

Figure 3. a) The patellar reflex can be controlled. b) The pupil reflex cannot be controlled.

4 Fingerprints: An Unshared Trait

What's the Plan?

Let's look at and lift your fingerprints.

What You Do

WHAT YOU NEED:

• magnifying glass

• ink pad

• white paper

• white dish or saucer

• wide, clear plastic tape

1. Look at the underside of your fingertips. You'll see a pattern of lines (raised skin ridges). These are your fingerprints. Fingerprints have three basic patterns— arches, loops, and whorls—and combinations of the basic patterns. (Figure 4a).

2. Using a magnifying glass, look at all your fingerprints. Which patterns do you see? Are all your fingerprints the same?

3. Detectives often lift fingerprints they find at a crime scene. You, too, can lift a fingerprint. Place one of your index fingers on an ink pad. Press that finger against a piece of paper. Then press it against the center of a white dish or saucer.

4. Place a length of clear, wide plastic tape over the fingerprint you left on the dish. Be careful! Don't touch the fingerprint (Figure 4b).

5. Remove the tape. Place the tape on a sheet of white paper.

6. Compare the fingerprint you lifted with the fingertip you used to make it.

What's Going On?

Criminals often leave their fingerprints at a crime scene. The fingerprints can be lifted and compared with fingerprints on file or with those of a suspect. Fingerprints are valuable evidence because no two people have the same fingerprints. Although identical twins have the same DNA, their fingerprints are different.

Keep Exploring—If You Have More Time!

- Use an ink pad and white paper to make fingerprint records of different people's ten fingers. Then stage some make-believe robberies and see if you can identify the "thief."

- What are latent fingerprints? How are they found? How can they be lifted?

- Do toes have toe prints?

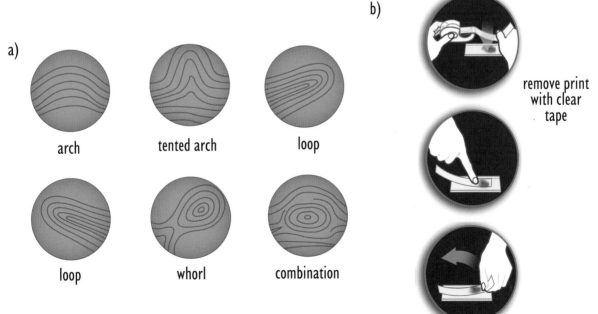

a)

arch   tented arch   loop

loop   whorl   combination

b)

remove print with clear tape

Figure 4. a) The common fingerprint patterns b) Lifting a fingerprint.

30 Minutes or Less

Really pressed for time? Here are some experiments you can do in 30 minutes or less.

5 How Many Hairs on a Human's Head?

What's the Plan?

Let's estimate the number of hairs on a human's head.

What You Do

1. Ask someone to let you examine and measure his or her head.

2. Place a metric ruler on the person's scalp. Count the number of hairs emerging from the scalp along a length of 1.0 cm (Figure 5a). Record that number.

3. Turn the ruler 90°. Again, count the number of hairs along a length of 1.0 cm perpendicular to the length you measured before. Record that number.

4. You can now find the number of hairs in one square centimeter (cm^2) of the person's head. Simply multiply the two numbers you recorded.

5. Using a cloth measuring tape, measure the circumference of the person's head. Record that length (Figure 5b).

> **WHAT YOU NEED:**
> - metric ruler
> - partner
> - cloth measuring tape
> - calculator (optional)
> - notebook
> - pencil

6. Assume the person's scalp is a hemisphere (half a sphere). Calculate the area of the person's scalp. To find the number of hairs, multiply the area by the number of hairs per square centimeter.

What's Going On?

Suppose you count 14 hairs along a centimeter and 13 hairs along the second centimeter. The number of hairs/cm^2 is 14 x 13 =182. If the circumference of the person's head is 56 cm, its diameter is approximately 18 cm because:

Diameter = Circumference/π = 56 cm/3.14 = 18 cm.

The head's radius is 9 cm (half the diameter), so the area of the person's scalp is:

Area of hemisphere = $2\pi r^2$
= 2 x 3.14 x 9 cm x 9 cm
= 509 cm^2

The number of hairs = number/cm^2 x area
= 182 hairs/cm^2 x 509 cm^2
= 92,638.

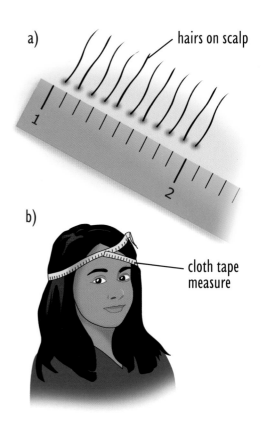

a) hairs on scalp

1

2

b)

cloth tape measure

Keep Exploring—If You Have More Time!

- Do blonds have more hair than brunettes? Than redheads?

- Do girls have more hairs on their scalps than boys?

Figure 5. a) Count the number of hairs along one centimeter of a person's scalp. b) Measure the circumference of that person's head. Assume the head is a hemisphere. Then the area of the scalp is $2\pi r^2$ where r (radius) is equal to circumference/2π.

6 Muscles Come in Pairs

What's the Plan?

Let's look at a pair of muscles that control your lower arm (Figure 6).

What You Do

1. Feel the muscle that bends your arm. Hold your left arm straight out. Put the palm of your right hand on the upper part of your left arm above the inside of your elbow.

> **WHAT YOU NEED:**
> • the muscles on your upper arm

2. Bend your left arm. As you do, the biceps muscle on the upper part of that arm contracts. Your right hand will feel your left biceps muscle contract and "make a muscle."

3. Repeat the experiment. This time put your fingers on the inside of your elbow. As your biceps contracts, feel the tendon that connects your biceps to the bones of your lower arm. The biceps pulls on the tendon, which, in turn, pulls on the lower arm bones. That pull raises your lower arm.

4. Put your right hand on the back of your bent left arm. Straighten your left arm slowly. Feel the triceps muscle on the back of the arm. Its contraction causes the arm to straighten.

5. Repeat the experiment. This time put your fingers on the back of your elbow. As your triceps contracts, feel the tendon that connects your triceps and pulls on the bones of your lower arm. That pull straightens your arm.

What's Going On?

Many of the muscles in our body are paired. For example, one muscle (the biceps) makes your arm bend at the elbow joint. Another (the triceps) causes your arm to straighten.

Keep Exploring—If You Have More Time!

- Do an experiment to determine the strength of your biceps versus that of your triceps.

- Do an experiment to measure the strength of the muscles that bend your leg versus those that straighten your leg. Are paired muscles equal in strength?

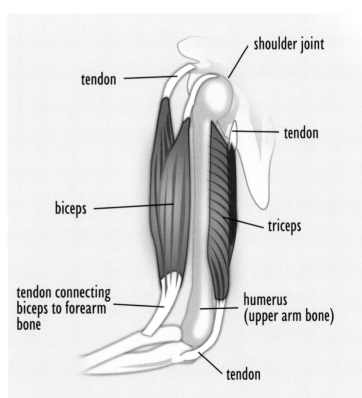

Figure 6. The biceps and triceps muscles move the lower arm. Muscles are connected to bones by tendons. When the biceps muscle contracts, it pulls the lower arm upward. When the triceps muscle contracts, it straightens the arm.

7 Look at Your Cells

What's the Plan?

Let's take a magnified look at some of the cells in your body.

What You Do

1. Place a drop of water on a microscope slide. **Under adult supervision**, add a drop of iodine to the water.

2. Using a toothpick, gently scrape the inside lining of your cheek. Some cheek cells will collect on the toothpick.

3. Mix the cheek cells with the water and iodine. Then discard the toothpick. **Do not put it back in your mouth! Iodine is poisonous.**

4. Carefully place a cover slip over the mixture of water, iodine, and cells (Figure 7).

5. Place the slide on the stage of a microscope. Look for cells on the slide using the high-power lens. You may be able to see the stained nucleus in some cells.

WHAT YOU NEED:

- an adult
- eyedropper
- water
- microscope slide
- cover slip
- toothpick
- iodine (tincture of iodine can be purchased at a pharmacy)
- microscope

What's Going On?

By scraping your cheek, you collected some of the epithelial cells on the lining of your cheek. You transferred some of those cells to the water and iodine on the slide. The iodine stained the cells, making them easier to see on the slide.

Keep Exploring—If You Have Time!

- Repeat the experiment but stain the cells with methylene blue instead of iodine. Does methylene blue make the cells easier to see?

- Under adult supervision, use the microscope, slides, and cover slips to look for single-celled animals and plants in pond water.

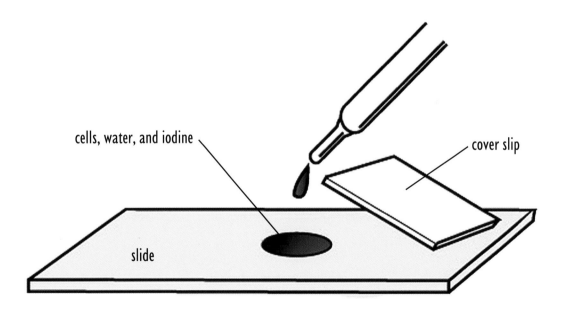

cells, water, and iodine

cover slip

slide

Figure 7. Make a slide of your cheek cells.

8 How We Breathe

What's the Plan?

Let's make a model to show how we breathe.

What You Do

WHAT YOU NEED:

- an adult
- knife or strong shears
- empty 2-liter, clear plastic soda bottle
- old balloon that has been inflated several times but does not leak
- clear plastic wrap
- large rubber bands
- clear plastic tape

1. Have an adult cut off the lower half of an empty 2-liter, clear plastic soda bottle.

2. Save the upper half. It represents your chest cavity.

3. Find an old balloon that has been inflated several times but does not leak.

4. Slip the neck of the balloon over the mouth of the bottle. Let the rest of the balloon hang inside the bottle, as shown in Figure 8. The balloon represents a lung.

5. Stretch clear plastic wrap over the open bottom of the bottle. Use large rubber bands to fasten the stretched plastic wrap to the bottle. The plastic wrap represents your diaphragm, the large muscle that separates your chest from your abdomen.

6. Cut a strip of clear plastic tape about 8 cm (3 in) long. Attach half the tape to the center of the plastic wrap. Hold the other half between two fingers. Hold the bottle with your other hand.

7. Use the strip of tape to pull the "diaphragm" downward. Watch the balloon (lung) expand.

8. When the "diaphragm" moves back up, air moves out of the balloon (lung).

What's Going On?

When the "diaphragm" moves down, the chest cavity expands. This makes the air pressure inside the chest cavity less than the air pressure outside. As a result, outside air moves into the "lung." When the diaphragm moves up, the chest cavity shrinks. The pressure in the lung becomes greater than the air pressure outside so air flows out of the lung.

Keep Exploring—If You Have More Time!

- Measure the circumference of a friend's chest when he inhales and when he exhales. Do your measurements agree with what you would expect according to the model?

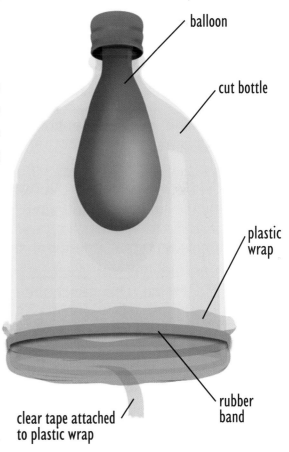

balloon

cut bottle

plastic wrap

rubber band

clear tape attached to plastic wrap

Figure 8. Make a model to show how we breathe. Expand the size of the chest cavity by moving the diaphragm downward. The real diaphragm is a large muscle that contracts to expand the chest cavity. Rib muscles also contract, helping make the chest larger.

9 How Much Air in a Breath?

What's the Plan?

Let's measure the air in one breath.

What You Do

1. Place a basin in a sink. Half fill the basin with cold water.

2. Fill a gallon jug with water. Ask an adult to cover the mouth of the jug and then invert it in the basin of water. Water will remain in the jug if its mouth is under the water.

3. Ask the adult to continue supporting the inverted jug.

4. Put the end of a piece of rubber tubing into the mouth of the jug (Figure 9a).

5. Inhale a normal amount of air. Then exhale a normal amount of air through the tubing into the jug. Then pinch the end of the tubing.

6. Ask the adult to use a marking pen to mark the water level in the jug after you have exhaled.

7. Inhale and exhale a normal amount of air. Then put the tubing back in your mouth and continue to exhale as much air as possible into the jug. Have the adult mark the new water level in the jug (Figure 9b).

WHAT YOU NEED:

- an adult
- wash basin
- sink
- cold water
- clear gallon jug
- rubber tubing about 1 ft (30 cm)
- long ruler
- marking pen
- graduated cylinder or metric measuring cup

8. Measure the air you exhaled in step 5. Then measure the extra air you exhaled in step 7 (Figure 9c).

What's Going On?

The air you normally inhale and exhale with each breath is called your tidal air. The extra air you can exhale is your supplemental air.

Keep Exploring—If You Have More Time!

- The total amount of air you can forcibly exhale after inhaling as much air as possible is your vital capacity. Find a way to measure your vital capacity.

- Even after forcibly exhaling as much air as possible, a residual volume of approximately 1.2 liters of air remains in your lungs. How could scientists measure the residual volume?

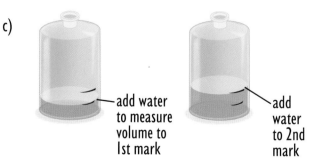

Figure 9. a) The normal volume of air exhaled can be measured by water displacement.
b) Supplemental air can be added to the volume of air normally exhaled. c) Both volumes can be measured by adding water to the marks on the empty jug.

25

10 Your Sense of Touch

What's the Plan?

Let's find out which parts of your body are most sensitive to touch.

What You Do

1 Hold two pencils against one another. Their sharpened points should both rest against a table (Figure 10a).

2. Tape the pencils together. **Keep the pencil points away from your eyes.**

WHAT YOU NEED:

• 3 pencils

• tape

• table

3. Which parts of your body can sense both touch points when they are so close together? Which will sense only one? To find out, gently touch the pencil tips against your lips, forehead, fingertips, thumb, palm, back of hand, forearm, and leg (Figure 10b).

4. Repeat the experiment, but this time place a third unsharpened pencil between the other two (Figure 10c). Then tape all three together. The touch points will now be twice as far apart.

What's Going On ?

Nerve receptors sensitive to touch are located in the skin all over your body. However, as you found, the receptors are farther apart in some places than in others. The touch receptors in your lips, tongue, and fingertips are abundant and close together. Because they are so abundant, you can detect two touch points that are very close together. Receptors on your arms, legs, and back are less abundant and farther apart. Consequently, two touch points may stimulate only one receptor. As a result, you feel only one touch not two. If the two touch points are farther apart, they may stimulate separate receptors so you feel two points on body parts that felt only one before.

Keep Exploring—If You Have More Time!

- Design and do experiments to locate receptors that respond to heat and cold in a partner's skin.

- Can any part of the human body, other than the eye, respond to light? Do an experiment to find out.

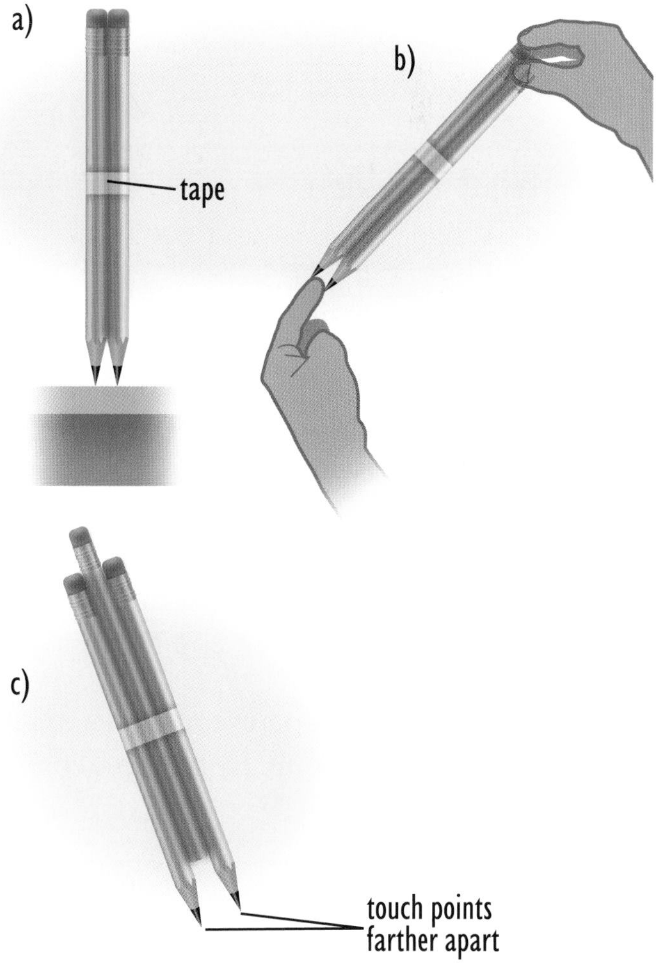

a)

b)

tape

c)

touch points farther apart

Figure 10. a) Tape two sharpened pencils together. b) Can your fingertips feel two touch points? How about other areas of your skin? c) Double the distance between the touch points. Tape a third unsharpened pencil between the first two.

15 Minutes or Less

Time is really in short supply if you need an experiment you can do in 15 minutes. Here to rescue you are five more experiments you can do quickly.

11 Is Gravity Needed to Drink or Eat?

What's the Plan?

Let's find out if the force of gravity is needed to swallow water or food.

What You Do

WHAT YOU NEED:
- drinking glass
- water
- drinking straw
- a parent or older sibling
- bread

1. Place a glass of water on the floor. Put a drinking straw in the water.

2. To see if gravity is needed to drink, try to drink while upside down. Ask a parent or older sibling to support your legs so that you are upside down (Figure 11).

3. Using the straw, try to drink the water while your stomach is well above your mouth. Were you successful?

4. Repeat the experiment with a small piece of bread. Can you swallow solid food without the help of gravity?

What's Going On?

When you swallow, muscles in your esophagus contract in a rhythmic way known as peristalsis. These contracting muscles force the solid foods or liquids along the esophagus and into the stomach. Peristalsis also moves food along the stomach and intestines.

Keep Exploring—If You Have More Time!

- Use a piece of rubber tubing to represent the esophagus. A marble can represent some food. Use these materials to show how peristalsis works.

- People working on the space station are in a weightless state. Do you think they eat off plates with forks and spoons? If not, how do you think they eat and drink?

Figure 11. Do you need gravity to drink? To eat?

29

12 The Colors of After Images

What's the Plan?

Let's stare at an image and then look at its after image.

What You Do

1. Stare at the colored flag in Figure 12 for at least 30 seconds. Then look at a white wall or a sheet of white paper. What you see is called an after image.

2. Describe the colors in the after image. Compare them with the colors in Figure 12.

What's Going On?

The colors you see in the after image are white dots on a blue background and stripes that are red and white. The colors in the after image are the complementary colors of those in the flag. The colors and their complementary colors are shown in the chart below.

Color in Flag	Complementary Color
black	white
yellow	blue
cyan	red

When you stare at the flag, there are cells, called cone cells, in the retina of your eye that respond to the specific primary colors of light—red, blue, and green. (White light is a combination of the primary colors of light.) These cells become tired after you stare at the same colors for a long time.

When you look at the white background, the cells that are not tired respond. They are the groups of cells sensitive to colors that create the complementary colors of black, yellow, and cyan—namely, white, blue, and red.

Keep Exploring—If You Have More Time!

- Under adult supervision, connect red, blue, and green lightbulbs in light sockets to an electrical outlet. Mix the colored lights by letting two or three at a time shine on a white wall. Which combination of colored lights produces yellow? Cyan (blue-green)? Magenta (purple)? White?

- Using the same colored lights, investigate the color of shadows made by shining these lights on a vertical stick in front of a white wall.

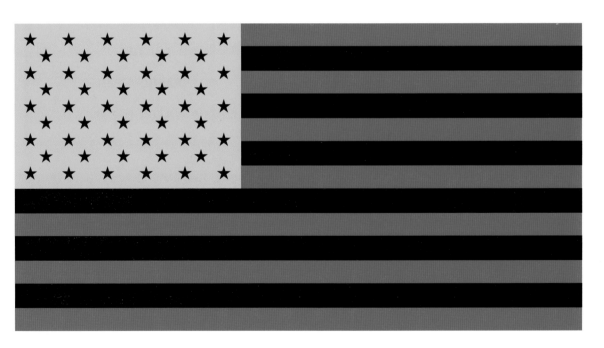

Figure 12. Stare at the flag for 30 seconds. Then look at a white wall or white paper. You will see an after image of the flag. What are the flag's colors in the after image?

13 Vision with a Cataract

What's the Plan

Normally the lens of a human eye is transparent. A cataract, which is common in older people but may occur even in babies, has many causes. The result is an increasingly cloudy lens. Let's find out how a cataract affects vision.

What You Do

1. The lens in your eye is similar to the convex lens (Figure 13a) found in a magnifying glass or telescope. Your eye lens, together with your cornea, bends light to form images that fall on your retina (Figure 13b).

2. You can see how this happens. Hold a convex lens near a light-colored wall opposite a window that opens onto a pleasant view. Move the lens toward and away from the wall until you get a clear image of the scene outside (Figure 13c).

3. To simulate the effect of an early cataract, ask a partner to hold a smooth piece of plastic wrap in front of the lens. Look at the image.

4. To simulate a more advanced cataract, hold a smooth piece of waxed paper in front of the lens. Look at the image.

What's Going On?

A cataract acts like plastic wrap or waxed paper in front of a lens. It reduces the amount of light passing through the lens and reaching the retina. As a result, the image on the retina is dimmer and less colorful.

Fortunately, surgery can cure this visual defect. The affected lens is removed and an artificial lens inserted. The operation is almost 100 percent effective.

Keep Exploring—If You Have More Time!

- As you saw, the images on the wall (and on a retina) are upside down. Try to explain why.

- Use two convex lenses to make a telescope or a microscope.

a)

b)

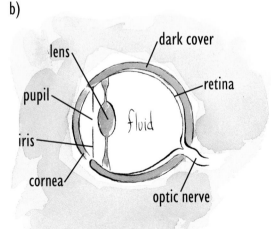

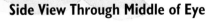

Side View Through Middle of Eye

c)

Figure 13. a) A convex lens can be found in a magnifying glass. b) A drawing of the human eye. c) Form an image on a wall using a convex lens. What happens to the image when you add a "cataract"?

14 Where's Your Blind Spot?

What's the Plan?

Let's find your blind spot. We all have one.

WHAT YOU NEED:
- white file card
- pen with black ink
- ruler

What You Do

1. On a white file card, make a small black circle with a diameter of about half a centimeter (1/4 in). Fill the circle with black ink.

2. About 8 cm (3 in) to the right of the circle, make a thick "X." The X should be about the same size as the circle (Figure 14a).

3. Close your left eye. Hold the card at arm's length directly in front of your right eye. Fix your eye on the circle. Slowly move the card toward your right eye. You will find a point at which the X disappears. It reappears when you move the card closer to your eye.

4. Repeat the experiment with your right eye closed. This time fix your left eye on the X. Slowly move the card toward your left eye. At some point, the circle will disappear.

What's Going On?

A small area of your retina, called the blind spot, has no cells that respond to light. It is where the fibers of the nerve cells sensitive to light come together (Figure 14b). They form the optic nerve that goes to the brain. If an image formed by your eye falls on that part of your retina, you cannot see it.

Keep Exploring—If You Have More Time!

- Figure out a way to measure the size of the blind spot on your retina. Then measure it. How large is it?

- Design and do an experiment to show that people can see colored images when they fall on the central part of the retina but not when they lie on the outer parts of the retina.

a)

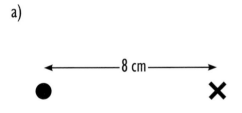

b)

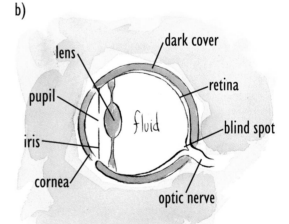

Figure 14. a) Circle and X used to find your blind spot. b) The location of the blind spot is shown in this diagram of the human eye.

Side View Through Middle of Eye

15 Listen to Your Heart

What's the Plan?

Let's listen to a heart.

What You Do

1. If you have a stethoscope, you can listen to your heart. Put both ear tips in your ears.

2 Place the chest piece slightly to the left of your chest's center. Move it until you hear distinct sounds. Listen for two sounds close together—a long booming sound followed by a short, sharp sound. Together they sound like "lubb-dup."

3. You'll hear the same sounds by placing your ear against a partner's chest.

4. While listening, count the number of times the heart beats in one minute. Does it agree with the count you can measure by taking a pulse? The number of times your heart beats in one minute is your heart rate (beats/minute). What is your heart rate?

5. Listen to your heart at the same time that you feel your pulse. Do they occur at the same time, or does one precede the other?

> **WHAT YOU NEED:**
> - stethoscope or a partner
> - watch or clock that can measure seconds

What's Going On?

The "lubb" is caused by the contracting heart muscle and the closing of the valves between the atria and ventricles (Figure 15). The "dup" is the sound of the aortic and pulmonary valves slamming shut as the heart relaxes. When

the heart muscle relaxes, blood tries to flow back into the heart. However, the valves between the ventricles and the aorta and pulmonary arteries are like a door to a room. They open only one way (out, into the arteries). When the blood tries to flow back to the heart, the valves slam shut with a loud "dup" sound.

A wrist pulse is several feet from the heart, so it follows the beat.

Keep Exploring—If You Have More Time!

- Do experiments to see how exercise and body position (standing, sitting, lying down) affect someone's heart rate.

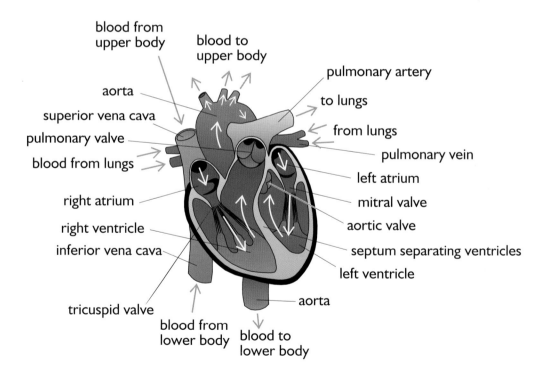

Figure 15. This diagram shows how blood passes to and from the heart. The contracting heart muscle and the heart's closing valves create the "lubb-dup" sound of the heartbeat.

5 Minutes or Less

Are you desperate? Do you have very little time to prepare a project? If so, you have come to the right place. Here are experiments you can do in five minutes or less.

16 Finding the Valves in Veins

What's the Plan?

Let's look for a valve in a vein.

What You Do

1. Many veins are near your body's surface. Their bluish color is visible through your skin. Sometimes they bulge above the skin on the back of your hand or the inside of your forearm.

> **WHAT YOU NEED:**
> • back of your hand or forearm where veins can be seen clearly

2. If you can't see a vein, let your arm hang down for 20 seconds. Blood will collect in the veins.

3. Once you see a vein clearly, put your index finger on it. Then "sweep" the blood in the vein toward your heart by moving the thumb of the same hand along the vein. When you reach a valve, the vein below the valve will collapse and become difficult to see (Figure 16a). You can see the blood-filled vein above the valve but not below it. Release your thumb and blood will flow through the vein again.

4. See if you can locate the next valve along the vein.

What's Going On?

Blood pumped from the heart passes through arteries and then tiny capillaries that lead to veins (Figure 16b). Veins carry blood back to the heart. The pressure in veins is much less than in arteries. In fact, without muscles squeezing the veins, blood would collect in the veins of the lower body. Blood flow is aided by the veins' one-way valves. These valves allow blood to move only one way—toward the heart.

Keep Exploring—If You Have More Time!

- Let your hand hang by your side until you can see the veins on the back of the hand. Raise that hand well above your heart. What happens to the veins? Can you explain why?

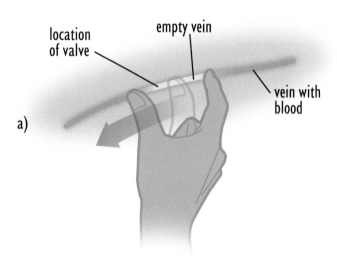

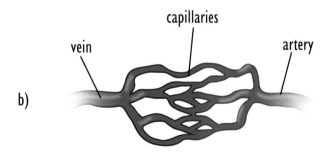

Figure 16. a) Locate a valve in a vein.
b) Capillaries are tiny vessels that connect arteries with veins.

17 How Fast Can You React?

WHAT YOU NEED:

• partner

• table

• yardstick

What's the Plan?

Let's find your reaction time.

What You Do

1. Rest your hand on the edge of a table with your thumb and fingers about 3 cm (1 in) apart. (Figure 17).

2. Your partner will hold a yardstick, which he will drop. The zero end of the stick should be even with your thumb and index finger.

3. Watch the bottom of the ruler. When your partner releases the stick, you will see the end of the ruler begin to fall. When you see it begin to fall, bring your thumb and fingers together. How far did the ruler fall before you caught it? The faster you react, the shorter the distance the ruler will fall.

4. To find your reaction time, use the table below. Record your reaction time. If you catch the ruler at a distance not in the table, you will have to estimate the time.

5. Repeat the experiment four times. Then calculate your average reaction time.

Distance stick fell (inches)	Reaction time (seconds)	Distance stick fell (inches)	Reaction time (seconds)
3	0.125	15	0.28
6	0.177	20	0.32
8	0.204	24	0.35
10	0.228	30	0.40
12	0.250	36	0.43

What's Going On?

Your reaction time is the time for a visual nerve stimulus to move from your eye to your brain and other nerve stimuli to travel from your brain to your forearm muscles.

Keep Exploring—If You Have More Time!

- Using a tape measure and the data you have collected, estimate the speed at which nerve impulses travel.

- Repeat the experiment. Test both hands. Does your dominant hand react faster than your other hand?

- Do experiments to find out whether age or gender affect reaction time.

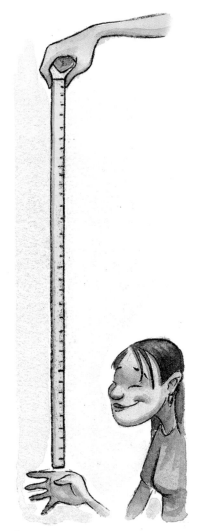

Figure 17. How fast can you react?

18 Taking Pulses

What's the Plan?

Let's learn how to take a human pulse.

What You Do

WHAT YOU NEED:
- your wrist
- watch that can measure seconds
- family members and friends

1. Put your first two fingers on the underside of your wrist just beyond the point where your thumb connects with your wrist (Figure 18). You should be able to feel a pulse (a brief expansion of the radial artery).

2. Count the number of pulses you feel during a 15-second period. Multiply that number by four to find your heart rate in beats per minute.

3. Measure the heart rate of your family and friends by taking their pulses.

What's Going On?

When your heart beats (contracts), it pushes blood into your main arteries. Arteries are elastic. They stretch like a rubber band when blood is pumped into them. They contract between heartbeats. When an artery is close to the body's surface, you can feel the artery pulsate (throb) with each heartbeat.

Keep Exploring—If You Have More Time!

- Amplify your pulse. Place your hand, palm upward, on a table. Put a small lump of clay on your pulse. Stick a straw upright in the clay. What happens to the straw each time your heart beats?

- Look for pulses in other places—either side of your Adam's apple, in front of your ear, and under your jaw. Where else can you feel a pulse?

- Take a partner's pulse at both his neck and wrist at the same time. Which pulse do you expect to feel first? Try it! Were you right?

- Do girls' hearts beat faster than boys'? Do older people have slower or faster heart rates than younger people?

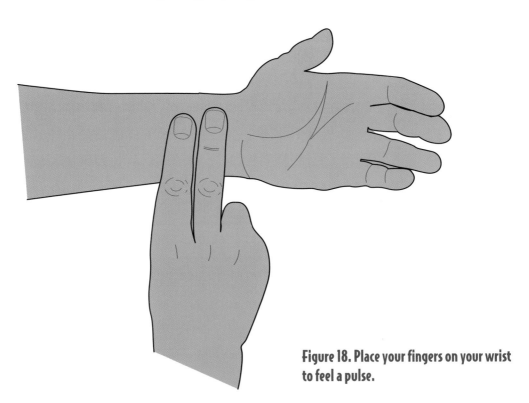

Figure 18. Place your fingers on your wrist to feel a pulse.

Words to Know

arteries—Blood vessels that carry blood away from the heart.

biceps—A muscle on the front of the upper arm. Its contraction raises the lower arm.

blind spot—A small area on the eye's retina where there are no cells that respond to light. In this region, there are only nerve fibers joining to form the optic nerve that goes to the brain.

capillaries—Tiny blood vessels that connect arteries to veins.

cataract—A defect that causes opacity (cloudiness) of the lens in the eye. As a result, images formed on the retina are dimmer and less colorful. In extreme cases, a cataract can cause blindness.

cell—The basic unit of living organisms, other than viruses. In the human body, cells are specialized for specific functions in body organs, such as the skin, heart, liver, brain, etc.

complementary color of light—The color of light added to another color that produces white light.

diaphragm—The large, sheetlike muscle that separates the chest from the abdomen.

exhale—Breathe air out of the lungs.

inhale—Breathe air into the lungs.

iodine—A chemical element that can be used to stain cells.

lever—A simple machine consisting of a rigid beam that turns on a pivot called the fulcrum. A force applied at one point on the lever is used to move a load at another point on the beam.

methylene blue—A chemical that is often used to stain cells.

peristalsis—Involuntary muscular contractions that travel along the digestive tract: the esophagus, stomach, and intestines.

primary colors of light—The colors of light (red, blue, and green) that can be combined to make all the other colors.

pulse—An expansion of an artery. The expansion is caused by the pressure created as the heart pushes blood into the main arteries. The expansion travels like a wave and can be felt at points where an artery is near the surface of the skin.

reflex—An unlearned response to a stimulus.

stethoscope—An instrument used to listen to the heart.

supplemental air—The extra volume of air you can force from your lungs after exhaling tidal air.

third-class lever—A lever, such as the human arm, in which both the weight (load) lifted and the force used to lift it are on the same side of the fulcrum. Also, in a third-class lever, the load is farther from the fulcrum than the force doing the lifting.

tidal air—The volume of air normally inhaled and exhaled during regular breathing.

triceps—A muscle on the back of the upper arm. Its contraction straightens the arm.

valves—Flap-like structures in the heart and veins that allow blood to pass in only one direction.

veins—Blood vessels that carry blood to the heart.

Further Reading

Books

Arnold, Nick. *Blood, Bones and Body Bits*. Toronto: Scholastic Canada, 2008.

Bardhan-Quallen, Sudipta. *Championship Science Fair Projects: 100 Sure-to-Win Experiments*. New York: Sterling, 2005.

Bochinski, Julianne Blair. *More Award-Winning Science Fair Projects*. Hoboken, N.J.:, John Wiley and Sons, 2004.

Ganeri, Anita. *Alive: The Living Breathing Human Body Book*. New York: DK Publishing, 2007.

Levine, Shar, and Leslie Johnstone. *First Science Experiments: The Amazing Human Body.* New York: Sterling Pub. Co., 2006.

Rhatigan, Joe, and Rain Newcomb. *Prize-Winning Science Fair Projects for Curious Kids.* New York: Lark Books, 2006.

Walker, Richard. *Human Body*. New York: DK Publishing, 2009.

Internet Addresses

Human Body for Kids

    <www.sciencekids.co.nz/humanbody.html>

Kids Science Projects

    <www.sciencemadesimple.com/projects.html>

Skeletal System

    <42explore.com/skeleton.htm>

Index